Also by Diana Kizlauskas:

LETTUCE!

CHRISTMAS BEST

www.brightbearbooks.com

ISBN: 978-0-9915233-8-2

A BULLY-BAD DAY

Written
and illustrated by

DIANA KIZLAUSKAS

BRIGHT BEAR BOOKS

To Stanley's family and friends

There's a *thud* outside the window,
then a *thump* and *swish*.
Stanley barks and I get worried.
What's that *squawk* and *squish*?

There's a pink flamingo dumping
Stanley's water bowl.
There's a panda squeezing Teddy.
Now he has a hole.

There's a big parade of critters
coming through the door.
It's a scene that we have never,
ever seen before!

There are parrots in the hallway,
flying through the air.
There are parrots on the staircase
and on every stair.

There are parrots on my shoulders,
parrots in my hair.
There are parrots crunching crackers —
feathers everywhere!

There's a bear in our recliner,
rude as he can be.
"This is *my* den," he announces,
"and it's *my* TV."

There's a hippo in the bathtub,
pouring out shampoo.
"Lots and lots for *me*," he giggles.
"No more left for *you*!"

There's a zebra in the closet,
wearing my best hat.
"I look great in stripes," he tells me.
"Stripes make *you* look fat."

There's a tiger in my bedroom,
swinging my new bat.
"You're no *dog*," he teases Stanley.
You're a fraidy-*cat*!"

There's a another group that's shouting,
"We won't let you play!"
There's an elephant that's cheering,
"Bullies, bullies, YAY!"

There's a kangaroo that's clucking,
"What a shame — oh, my!
It's no wonder you can't catch me.
You can't jump this high."

There's a tortoise in our kitchen,
throwing globs of jam.
"Berries taste too sweet," he grumbles.
"I want eggs and ham."

There's a squid inside our washer
squirting jets of ink.
There's an armadillo singing,
"You and Stanley stink."

"That's a nasty song," I answer.
"None of it is true.
And we *don't* want loads of laundry
turning black and blue!"

"Listen up," I tell the bullies,
"we have had ENOUGH!
Please respect our things and feelings.
Don't be mean and rough."

But they all refuse to hear it.
They won't let me be.
They just keep on misbehaving
and make fun of me.

Then I hear what sounds like thunder:
rumble, *roar* and *BOOM*.
There's a lion on the sofa
in the living room!

I can see him lifting Stanley.
Stanley shakes with fear.
"Move along, you mutt," he threatens,
"or I'll bite your ear."

I jump in to save my Stanley.
We run off to hide.
We find boxes in the attic
and we crawl inside.

"This is more than bad," I whisper.
"This is **bully**-bad!
This will take a lot of thinking.
Hush now, don't be sad."

Should we act like nothing happened?
...wish them all away?
Should we pack and move to Grandma's?
...let the bullies stay?

Should we beg them to be nicer?
...take them out to lunch?
Should we give them gifts to stop this?
Should we throw a punch?

"Bad ideas," I tell Stanley.
"We should think some more.
Stuff up here might give us answers.
Go ahead, explore."

Soon we find Great-grandpa's suitcase,
left here long ago.
His awards and letters tell us
special things to know.

"Stan, that's *it*! This calls for teamwork.
Time to make our play.
"We need **help** to win this battle.
Go, boy! Lead the way!"

So, we run back down the stairway
(past a kicking mule)
and we look out on the terrace,
where it's calm and cool.

There they are! We see our family.
That's our winning team.
As I slide the back door open,
Stanley yelps, I scream.

"We need HELP!" I yell. "There's trouble!"
They know what to do.
They call up the people working
at the City Zoo.

Doctor Wilson comes right over
and she brings her crew.
Then she takes some time to teach us
things we never knew.

"There are many different reasons
for what bullies do."
She explains, "They need direction —
understanding, too."

"Bullies often come from settings
where they're scared and sad.
Being treated very badly
makes them mean and mad.

They need hugs and gentle handling.
They need food to eat.
Some need help to be less selfish
and to be more neat.

TEST LAB 2

TEST LAB 3

BATH RULES
- NO SPLASHING
- SOAP LIMIT: 1cup
- WAIT YOUR TURN
- NO NAME-CALLING
BE KIND

Some must learn to be less bossy.
Some need lots of space.
Others need the warmth and comfort
of a safer place.

While the ones who mean real danger
need to live apart,
some just need a bit of urging
and a brand new start."

"Come with us," she calls the bullies.
"There's a home for you.
You'll be getting what you're missing
at the City Zoo."

All the bullies crowd the zoo bus.
What a silly sight!
As the sun goes down, we watch them
ride into the night.

We imagine how the bullies

After all, they're busy learning
how to love and share.
We stop by the zoo to visit.
They can see we care.

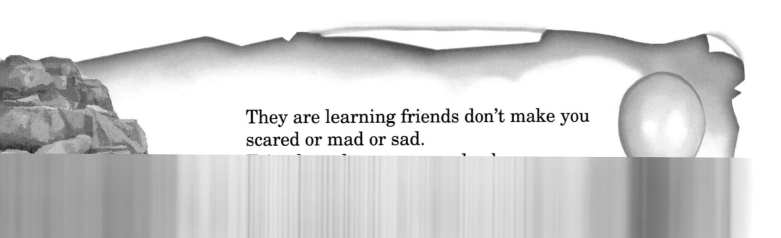

They are learning friends don't make you
scared or mad or sad.

RESOURCES

ONLINE

HOW TO HANDLE PRESCHOOL BULLIES – Parenting
https://www.parenting.com/toddler/how-to-handle-preschool-bullies

PREVENTING BULLYING IN EARLY CHILDHOOD – EDC PromotePrevent
http://preventingbullying.promoteprevent.org/preventing-bullying-in-early
-childhood

BULLYING IN PRESCHOOL: WHAT PARENTS NEED TO KNOW – Education.com
https://www.education.com/magazine/article/bullying-preschool/

HOW TO DEAL WITH BULLIES: A GUIDE FOR PARENTS – Parents Magazine
https://www.parents.com/kids/problems/bullying/bully-proof-your-child-how-
to-deal-with-bullies/

BULLYING AT PRESCHOOL: HELPING YOUR CHILD
– Raising Children Network
https://raisingchildren.net.au/preschoolers/behaviour
/bullying/preschool-bullying-helping

BOOKS

Donovan, Sandy. *How Can I Deal with Bullying? A Book about Respec*t. Minneapolis: Lerner Publications, 2014.

Genhart, Michael. *Ouch! Moments: When Words Are Used in Hurtful Ways.* Washington, D.C.: Magination Press,2016.

Sornson, Bob and Maria Dismondy. *Juice Box Bully: Empowering Kids to Stand Up for Others.* Northville, MI: Ferne Press, 2010.

AUTHOR'S NOTE

[illegible]

    - run for safety, if necessary.
    - ask parents, guardians or teachers for help with the problem.
If a bullying problem exists, parents are advised to:
    - involve teachers or other authority figures and the offending child's family in
      working through the situation.
    - help the victimized child maintain a sense of self-worth.
    - help their child keep a positive outlook regarding peer relationships.

    A BULLY-BAD DAY is a whimsical, symbolic story informed by this guidance. It was written to encourage children to think about and discuss bullying with the adults in their lives. The comical crew of critters that invades the little boy's home presents a variety of bullying behaviors — *physical, social* and *emotional* — for children to examine. Young readers join the main characters' search to find a solution to their bully-bad dilemma and are led to the main message of this tall tale: when the bully will not back away, *GET HELP!* As Dr. Wilson saves the day, she also presents reasons for a bully's bad behavior, suggesting that our two heroes (and readers) bring patience, understanding and compassion to the very complex situation. I truly hope that my readers never encounter more than the silly ruffians that fill these pages. But if they do find that they are the victims of a bully, observe bullying, or are, in fact, *the* bully, I hope that insights gathered from this story will help them address the problem successfully.

DIANA KIZLAUSKAS is a Chicago area artist whose children's illustrations have been published by Harcourt Achieve, Macmillan McGraw-Hill, Pearson Education/Scott Foresman, Compass/Seed Media, Pauline Books & Media, EDCO/Ireland and other internationally known companies. She has written and illustrated *LETTUCE!* (2015) and *CHRISTMAS BEST* (2016), two picture books published independently under the imprint of Bright Bear Books. She is a Society of Children's Book Writers and Illustrators PAL member. Diana's formal training includes BA degrees in Illustration and Art Education. Besides advertising, editorial and children's illustration, her work experience includes PreK-2 teaching. She has two children, two grandchildren and two very sweet and cuddly granddogs.

STANLEY is a friendly labradoodle who lives in Florida. He is a proud graduate of several training programs and is a brave protector of home and family. He loves swimming, playing with children, chewing his toys, zooming around the backyard and visiting with his Nana D.

See more of Diana's work at:
www.dianakizlauskas.com